A £1.00

THE NATURAL COOK

THE
NATURAL
COOK

Exciting recipes for healthy eating

SACKVILLE BOOKS

First published in 1987
by Sackville Books Ltd
Sackville House
78 Margaret Street, London W1N 7HB

© Sackville Design Group Ltd 1987

Designed and produced by Sackville Design Group Ltd
Typeset in Bembo by Bookworm Typesetting Ltd, Manchester

Art director: Al Rockall
Editor: Lorraine Jerram
Photographs: Sue Jorgensen

British Library Cataloguing in Publication Data
Rhodes, Lorna
The natural cook: exciting recipes for healthy eating.
1. Cookery (Natural foods)
I. Title   II. Bampfylde, Zune
641.5'637   TX741

ISBN 0–948615–08–7

Printed and bound in Spain by Graficas Estella, S.A. Navarra

Notes on recipes
1 All the recipes are to serve 4 people only unless otherwise specified.
2 All herbs used are fresh.
3 All eggs are size 3.

Contents

Introduction

Nowadays, most people have an awareness of the accepted healthy eating formula: more fibre, fewer refined carbohydrates, less fat. However, many are put off by the 'wholefoods' image that has accompanied this eating revolution. They believe that being diet-conscious means sacrificing variety and taste. They are mistaken. *The Natural Cook* shows you that a fresh approach to cooking natural ingredients, with nothing added and nothing taken away, is all you really need to discover how easy it is to prepare truly exciting healthy dishes.

The recipes in this book embrace all aspects of healthy eating, capitalizing on the positive steps that have already been taken towards a healthier, more varied diet. For example, the availability of natural ingredients has grown rapidly in recent years, particularly the low-fat, reduced sugar, reduced salt, high-fibre vegetarian alternatives to traditional foods. Similarly, there has been a tremendous increase in the number and types of fresh fruit and vegetables available; not only are these delicious and interesting to cook, but they contribute fibre as well as essential vitamins and minerals to our diet. The sight of gleaming fruit and vegetable displays on market stalls and in supermarkets provides continual inspiration for the use of natural foods in everyday cooking, foods which enable you to make the most of your creative flair.

As well as high-fibre unrefined carbohydrates, such as wholegrain cereals, pulses, beans, fruit and vegetables, *The Natural Cook* makes extensive use of fresh herbs for flavouring (but dried herbs can be substituted if fresh are not available). Herbs, spices and other seasonings are a viable alternative to salt, which most of us consume in greater quantities than we need or is good for us. The recipe ideas in this book encourage you to experiment with flavourings – only add the very minimum of sea salt after tasting when the recipe says 'season'.

Fats, particularly saturated fats, have also been cut down or replaced by unsaturated fats and oils. Sunflower and olive oil are used throughout – olive oil contributes an authentic flavour to many ethnic dishes – but you can choose the variety to suit your palate. You are also encouraged to adopt a more healthy approach to eating meat, especially red meat, and are recommended to choose only the leanest cuts and preferably poultry and fish.

Eating a sensible, healthy diet need not be dull or unadventurous. *The Natural Cook* shows you how colourful, enjoyable and interesting natural foods can be when prepared and presented with a little imagination. Quick and easy to prepare, there are recipe ideas for every occasion, some traditional and some with a distinctly international flavour, so that providing family and friends with well-balanced meals becomes a sheer delight. Cooking and eating the natural way will bring out the natural cook in you.

Snacks & Starters

*Cool green asparagus mousse makes an
irresistibly light and refreshing first course.*

Asparagus mousse

450g/1lb fresh asparagus
45ml/3 tablespoons chicken stock
15g/½oz gelatine
225g/8oz fromage frais (low-fat soft cheese)
salt and freshly ground black pepper
2 egg whites
Garnish
curly endive
30ml/2 tablespoons natural yoghurt
sprigs of watercress

Trim away the woody parts from the asparagus tips and cut the stalks into 5cm/2in lengths. Simmer in a pan with 150ml/¼ pint water for about 7 minutes or until tender. Reserve a few tips for the garnish and purée the rest in a blender with 45ml/3 tablespoons of the cooking liquor.

Pour the stock into a small bowl, sprinkle over the gelatine and allow to become spongy. Place in a pan of simmering water and stir until dissolved. Turn the purée into a bowl, stir in the gelatine, then beat in the fromage frais and season. Refrigerate until the mixture begins to thicken. Whisk the egg whites until stiff, then fold into the mixture. Pour the mousse into 6 individual ramekin dishes and refrigerate until set.

Turn out on to plates and garnish with endive and the reserved asparagus tips. Spoon a little yoghurt on to each mousse and finish with a sprig of watercress.

Serves 6

*T*angy tomato rings complemented by a thick
pesto sauce conjure up the taste of summer.

Tomato rings with basil sauce

450g/1lb tomatoes, chopped
1 small onion, chopped
1 clove garlic, crushed
2.5ml/½ teaspoon celery salt
5ml/1 teaspoon tomato purée
5ml/1 teaspoon white wine vinegar
15g/½oz gelatine
Sauce
50g/2oz fresh basil leaves
50g/2oz pine nuts, lightly toasted
1 clove garlic, crushed
125ml/4floz olive oil
50g/2oz freshly grated Parmesan cheese
salt and freshly ground black pepper
60ml/4 tablespoons single cream
Garnish
cucumber slices
basil leaves

Simmer the tomatoes, onion, garlic, celery salt, tomato purée and vinegar in a saucepan until soft and pulpy. Sieve into a 600ml/1 pint measuring jug. Pour 60ml/4 tablespoons into a small bowl, sprinkle over the gelatine and leave to become spongy. Dissolve over a pan of simmering water, then allow to cool and stir into the tomato purée, making up to 600ml/1 pint if necessary. Pour the mixture into four individual ring moulds and refrigerate until set.

Wash and dry the basil leaves, then work in a blender or food processor with the pine nuts, garlic and olive oil until the mixture is thick and smooth. Turn out into a bowl, beat in the cheese and season.

Turn the tomato rings out on to plates and arrange halved cucumber slices around the edge. Mix half the pesto sauce with the cream, then spoon into the centre of each ring. Garnish with basil leaves before serving. (The rest of the pesto sauce can be stored in the refrigerator.)

*A*ubergine, rich tomato sauce and Mozzarella cheese
make this an appetizing supper dish from southern Italy.

Melanzane alla Parmigiana

2 aubergines, sliced
90ml/6 tablespoons olive oil
1 onion, chopped
400g/14oz can tomatoes, roughly-chopped
15ml/1 tablespoon tomato purée
5ml/1 teaspoon sugar
5ml/1 teaspoon chopped basil or oregano
salt and freshly ground black pepper
30ml/2 tablespoons wholemeal flour
175g/6oz Mozzarella cheese, thinly sliced
25g/1oz Parmesan cheese, grated
Garnish
basil leaves

Put the sliced aubergine into a colander, sprinkle with salt, and set aside for 30 minutes. Heat 30ml/2 table-spoons of the oil in a pan, then add the onion and cook until soft. Stir in the tomatoes, tomato purée, sugar and basil, and season. Bring to the boil and simmer for 20 minutes. Rinse and dry the aubergine slices, dust with the flour, then fry in the remaining oil until golden brown. Drain on absorbent paper.

Place a layer of aubergines across the base of an ovenproof dish, followed by a layer of tomato sauce and a layer of Mozzarella cheese; sprinkle lightly with Parmesan. Repeat these layers, then add a final layer of aubergine.

Sprinkle with the rest of the Parmesan and bake at 190°C/375°F/gas 5 for about 30 minutes until golden brown and bubbling.

This classic French dish flavoured with saffron, fresh herbs and orange peel captures the scent of the Mediterranean.

16

Bouillabaisse

1kg/2lb mixed fish, e.g. monkfish, cod, mullet, squid, whiting
450g/1lb shellfish, e.g. prawns, mussels, langoustines
30ml/2 tablespoons olive oil
1 large onion, chopped
1 bulb fennel, sliced
2 cloves garlic, crushed
2 medium-size potatoes, diced
4 tomatoes, skinned and chopped
2–3 sprigs of parsley
good pinch of saffron threads
few strips of orange peel
1.2 litres/2 pints water
salt and freshly ground black pepper
Garnish
freshly chopped parsley

Clean and prepare the fish, removing the skin and bones and cutting into chunks. The shellfish can be left in their shells, although the heads may be removed if desired. Heat the oil in a large saucepan and add the onion, fennel and garlic. Cook over a gentle heat for 10 minutes.

Add the white firmer fish, potatoes, tomatoes, parsley sprigs, saffron and orange peel. Pour in the water and season with salt and pepper. Bring to the boil, then simmer for 15 minutes. Add the shellfish and cook for a further 5 minutes.

Serve sprinkled with the chopped parsley.

Nutty parsnip soup

15g/½oz sunflower margarine
450g/1lb parsnips, chopped
1 onion, chopped
5ml/1 teaspoon mild curry powder
900ml/1½ pints vegetable stock
50g/2oz finely chopped walnuts
salt and freshly ground black pepper
5ml/1 teaspoon soft brown sugar
300ml/½ pint semi-skimmed milk
Garnish
chopped parsley

Melt the margarine in a saucepan, add the vegetables and cook gently over a low heat until softened and tender. Stir in the curry powder and cook for 2–3 minutes. Add the stock, walnuts, seasoning and sugar and bring to the boil. Reduce the heat to simmer, cover and cook gently for 15 minutes until the vegetables are tender. Liquidize and return to the pan. Add the milk, then heat through gently and serve garnished with chopped parsley.

Red pepper soup

3 red peppers, seeded and chopped
1 medium-size onion, chopped
1 clove garlic, crushed
30ml/2 tablespoons olive oil
225g/8oz ripe tomatoes, skinned and chopped
900ml/1½ pints chicken stock
9 basil leaves, shredded
salt and freshly ground black pepper
pinch of cayenne
To serve
100g/4oz crème fraîche or soured cream

Put the peppers, onion, garlic and oil into a saucepan and cook gently until the onion is soft. Add the tomatoes and stock, and bring to the boil. Then add the basil and seasoning and simmer for 20 minutes. Liquidize in a blender or food processor then sieve the soup, pressing the vegetables through. Discard the skin left in the sieve.

Re-heat the soup before serving, spooning a table-spoon of crème fraîche on to each portion.

*F*illed with crabmeat and shrimps, and baked until golden brown, hot avocado makes a delicious first course.

Baked avocado with seafood sauce

*2 large avocados
juice of ½ lemon
25g/1oz butter
5ml/1 teaspoon mild curry powder
25g/1oz wholemeal flour
210ml/7floz semi-skimmed milk
75g/3oz cooked or canned crabmeat
50g/2oz peeled, cooked shrimps
25g/1oz Gruyère cheese, finely grated
salt and freshly ground black pepper
15ml/1 tablespoon grated Parmesan cheese
Garnish
small lemon wedges
chervil*

Heat the butter in a saucepan, stir in the curry powder and cook for 30 seconds. Stir in the flour, then blend in the milk. Bring to the boil, stirring all the time, and simmer for 1 minute. Allow to cool slightly before stirring in the crabmeat, shrimps and cheese, then season with salt and pepper.

Halve and stone the avocados and sprinkle with lemon juice. Scoop out and chop a little of the flesh, and gently fold into the filling. Divide the seafood filling between the avocado halves, sprinkle with Parmesan, and bake in a pre-heated oven at 190°C/375°F/gas 5 for 15 minutes. Place under a hot grill until golden.

Serve garnished with lemon wedges and chervil.

Pretty artichoke cases contain a light tuna and egg filling and are served with a tasty yoghurt and mustard dressing.

Stuffed globe artichokes

4 globe artichokes
½ lemon
200g/7oz can tuna, drained
100g/4oz low-fat soft cheese
4 hard-boiled eggs
15ml/1 tablespoon chopped parsley
salt and freshly ground black pepper
pinch of cayenne
Dressing
30ml/2 tablespoons olive oil
30ml/2 tablespoons sunflower oil
grated rind of 1 lemon
30ml/2 tablespoons lemon juice
15ml/1 tablespoon natural yoghurt
1 clove garlic, crushed
2.5ml/½ teaspoon Dijon mustard

Cut the stalk of each artichoke level with the base and remove any discoloured leaves. Snip the tips off the leaves and cut off the top quarter of each artichoke with a sharp knife. Rub the cut surfaces with the lemon. Plunge into a large saucepan of lightly salted water, then cover and simmer for 30–40 minutes until tender and a leaf comes away when pulled. Drain and leave to cool.

Work the tuna and soft cheese in a food processor until smooth. Add the eggs and process again until they are finely chopped. Stir in the parsley and season.

Remove some of the leaves from the centre of each artichoke and then scoop out the hairy choke. Fill with the tuna mixture. Stand each artichoke on a serving plate. Mix together the ingredients for the dressing and serve as an accompaniment.

*Two-coloured pasta with avocado sauce, ham and mushrooms
makes this an attractive starter or nutritious snack.*

Tagliatelle in avocado sauce

450g/1lb mixed green and yellow tagliatelle
30ml/2 tablespoons olive oil
1 shallot, finely chopped
100g/4oz button mushrooms, sliced
1 avocado, peeled and sliced
squeeze lemon juice
90ml/6 tablespoons single cream
100g/4oz cooked ham, diced
salt and freshly ground black pepper
pinch of nutmeg
To serve
freshly grated Parmesan cheese

Cook the pasta in plenty of boiling salted water until it is *al dente*. Drain and keep warm.

Heat the oil in the same large pan and cook the shallot and mushrooms quickly until tender. Scoop the avocado flesh into a bowl, mash together with the lemon juice, then beat in the cream. Add the ham, avocado sauce and seasonings, and heat through. Replace the pasta and heat gently, tossing it in the sauce. Pile on to serving plates and serve with the Parmesan to sprinkle over as desired.

Serves 6 as a starter

*S*trips of smoked salmon and mange-tout bites make this light and delicate dish a distinctive start to any meal.

Spaghetti with salmon and mange-tout

350g/12oz wholemeal spaghetti
15ml/1 tablespoon olive oil
1 small onion, chopped
175g/6oz mange-tout, trimmed
45ml/3 tablespoons single cream
pinch of ground nutmeg
salt and freshly ground black pepper
75g/3oz smoked salmon, cut into strips
15ml/1 tablespoon chopped parsley
To serve
grated Parmesan cheese

Cook the spaghetti in a large pan of boiling salted water until just tender. While it is cooking, heat the oil in another pan and gently cook the onion until soft. Cook the mange-tout for 2 minutes in boiling water, then drain.

Drain the spaghetti and return to the pan. Add the cooked onion and mange-tout and toss together. Then add the cream and nutmeg, and season with salt and pepper. Toss together and heat through for 1–2 minutes. Finally, add the salmon and parsley.

Serve immediately with the Parmesan cheese, which can be sprinkled over if desired.

Gnocchi verdi

450g/1lb spinach, washed and shredded
225g/8oz ricotta cheese
75g/3oz freshly grated Parmesan cheese
50g/2oz wholemeal flour
2 egg yolks
salt and freshly ground black pepper
40g/1½oz butter, melted

Cook the spinach in a little water for about 5 minutes until soft. Drain well until dry, then place in a blender and chop finely. Turn into a bowl and add the ricotta cheese, 50g/2oz of the Parmesan, the flour, egg yolks and seasoning, and then mix thoroughly.

With floured hands shape the mixture into balls about 1cm/½in in diameter and place on a floured tray. (The gnocchi can be covered and refrigerated until needed.)

Drop the gnocchi one by one into a large pan of simmering salted water and cook for 3–4 minutes. Since they float to the surface you will need to cook them in 2 or 3 batches. Remove with a slotted spoon and keep warm while cooking the next batch.

Divide the cooked gnocchi between four ovenproof serving dishes. Dribble over the melted butter, sprinkle the remaining Parmesan on top, then place under a hot grill until the cheese melts.

Mushroom pâté

40g/1½oz butter
1 shallot, finely chopped
225g/8oz flat mushrooms, finely chopped
100g/4oz quark or low-fat soft cheese
40g/1½oz fresh wholemeal breadcrumbs
10ml/2 teaspoons mushroom ketchup
salt and freshly ground black pepper

Melt the butter in a frying pan, then add the shallot and cook until soft. Squeeze the chopped mushrooms in absorbent paper to remove any excess liquid, then add to the shallot and cook over a low heat for 10 minutes or until the liquid has evaporated.

Put the mushrooms into a blender or food processor with the rest of the ingredients and work to a rough purée. Spoon the pâté into a serving dish and chill for at least 4 hours, or overnight, before serving.

These Chinese dumplings are filled with minced pork and served with a spicy sauce for an authentic Oriental mood.

Chinese crescents

50g/2oz plain flour
75g/3oz wholemeal flour
125ml/4floz boiling water
30ml/2 tablespoons sunflower oil
Filling
175g/6oz minced pork
25g/1oz water chestnuts, finely chopped
4 spring onions, finely chopped
5ml/1 teaspoon finely chopped ginger
15ml/1 tablespoon dry sherry
15ml/1 tablespoon dark soy sauce
salt
pinch of sugar
Sauce
15ml/1 tablespoon Hoisin sauce
15ml/1 tablespoon soy sauce
15ml/1 tablespoon water
Garnish
spring onion tassels

Mix together the flours and water to make a smooth dough. Turn out on to a floured surface and knead for 2–3 minutes. Put in a bowl, cover and leave to rest for 2 minutes. Mix together the ingredients for the filling.

Roll out the dough to make a long sausage, then cut into 18 pieces. Roll each piece into a circle about 6cm/2½in in diameter. Place 1 teaspoon of filling on each pancake, dampen the edges, and fold in half. Press the edges together and pinch.

Heat the oil in a large frying pan, add the crescents flat side down, and cook over a low heat until golden. Pour over 150ml/¼ pint water, cover and cook for about 15 minutes until all the liquid is absorbed. Uncover and cook for a further 2 minutes. Mix together the ingredients for the sauce. Arrange three crescents on each plate and spoon a little of the sauce on to each. Serve garnished with spring onion tassels.

Serves 6

Russian buckwheat pancakes make a sophisticated first course when topped with red and black lumpfish.

Blinis with lumpfish

15g/½oz fresh yeast or
10ml/2 teaspoons dried yeast and pinch of sugar
300ml/½ pint tepid semi-skimmed milk
100g/4oz buckwheat flour
100g/4oz strong plain flour
1 egg, separated
30ml/2 tablespoons natural yoghurt
15ml/1 tablespoon oil
To serve
fromage frais (low-fat soft cheese)
red and black lumpfish
dill

Blend the fresh yeast with the milk. If using dried yeast, mix the milk with the sugar, sprinkle the yeast on top and leave for 15 minutes until frothy. Sift the flours into a mixing bowl. Add the yeast liquid and beat to a smooth batter. Beat in the egg yolk and yoghurt, cover and leave to rise in a warm place for 40 minutes.

Whisk the egg white until stiff and fold lightly into the batter. Heat a lightly-oiled frying pan over a medium heat and, when hot, drop spoonfuls of the batter, well-spaced apart, cooking about 3 blinis at a time. Cook for 2 minutes until the undersides are set and golden. Flip the blinis over and cook the other side. Keep them warm until all the batter has been used.

Spoon fromage frais on to each blini and arrange a spoonful of each lumpfish on top. Serve garnished with dill.

This refreshing dish uses fish marinated in fruit juices, oil, pepper and onion to give it a Latin American tang.

Fish escabeche

450g/1lh monkfish, skinned and boned
60ml/4 tablespoons olive oil
1 bay leaf
juice of 3 lemons or limes
juice of 2 oranges
1 orange, peeled and sliced
½ green pepper, seeded and finely chopped
4 spring onions, finely chopped
salt and freshly ground black pepper
Garnish
1 small avocado, peeled and sliced
75g/3oz peeled prawns
tiny sprigs of parsley

Cut the fillets of monkfish into small bite-sized pieces. Heat half the oil in a frying pan and cook the fish until it becomes firm. Remove with a slotted spoon and put into a shallow dish with the bay leaf. Pour over the fruit juices and remaining oil. Arrange the orange slices, scatter over the green pepper and spring onions, and season. Cover the dish and refrigerate for at least 12 hours.

Just before serving, remove the bay leaf. Spoon into individual dishes and garnish with the avocado slices, prawns and parsley.

Individual quiches look so attractive with their combination of herb pastry and smoked haddock and prawn filling.

Seafood quiche

100g/4oz sunflower margarine
100g/4oz wholemeal flour
100g/4oz plain flour
15ml/1 tablespoon chopped parsley
15ml/1 tablespoon chopped mixed herbs, e.g. chives, dill
225g/8oz undyed smoked haddock
100g/4oz peeled prawns
2 eggs
150ml/¼ pint semi-skimmed milk
salt and freshly ground black pepper
15ml/1 tablespoon chopped chives
25g/1oz Cheddar cheese, finely grated
Garnish
salad leaves
chives

Make the pastry by rubbing the margarine into the flours with a pinch of salt. Stir in the herbs, then bind together with a little cold water to make a smooth dough. Divide the pastry into four, then roll out and line four individual quiche tins. Chill for 30 minutes. Heat the oven to 200°C/400°F/gas 6. Prick the pastry cases with a fork, then line with foil and bake in the oven for 15 minutes.

Place the fish in a pan with a little water and poach for a few minutes until flaking. Remove from the liquid and flake the flesh into a bowl. Divide the haddock and prawns between the pastry cases. Beat the eggs and milk together and season. Pour over the fish, sprinkle with the chives and cheese, and bake in the oven for 15 minutes. Reduce to 180°C/350°F/gas 4 and cook until golden.

Serve hot or cold, garnished with a few salad leaves and chives.

Crab claws flavoured with ginger and Oriental sauce are an exotic starter for that special occasion.

Chinese crab claws

12 partly-shelled crab claws
30ml/2 tablespoons sunflower oil
2.5cm/1in piece ginger, finely chopped
1 clove garlic, crushed
½ bunch spring onions, chopped
1 small red pepper, seeded and finely sliced
45ml/3 tablespoons chicken stock
15ml/1 tablespoon dry sherry
15ml/1 tablespoon light soy sauce
10ml/2 teaspoons oyster sauce
5ml/1 teaspoon cornflour

Heat the oil in a frying pan. Add the crab claws, ginger, and garlic and cook over a medium heat for 2 minutes. Add the spring onions and pepper and cook for a further 2 minutes.

Pour in the stock, sherry, soy sauce and oyster sauce and cook over a gentle heat for 2–3 minutes. Remove the crab claws on to serving plates. Arrange the onions and peppers as a garnish, and keep warm. Blend the cornflour with a little water, then stir into the sauce and heat until thickened.

Spoon over the crab claws and serve.

Farmhouse fondue

½ small onion
250ml/8fl oz dry cider
5ml/1 teaspoon lemon juice
175g/6oz Cheddar cheese, grated
175g/6oz Red Leicester cheese, grated
2.5ml/½ teaspoon dry mustard
15ml/1 tablespoon cornflour
45ml/3 tablespoons apple juice
pepper
To serve
wedges of apple, sticks of celery, sticks of carrot

Put the onion and cider into a saucepan, heat until simmering then discard the onion. Add the lemon juice, then turn the heat to low and gradually stir in the cheeses. Continue to heat until the cheeses melt.

In a small bowl, blend the mustard and cornflour with the apple juice. Stir into the cheese mixture and continue to cook until the fondue is thick and creamy. Season with pepper. Pour into six small individual dishes and serve with the apple wedges, celery and carrot sticks to be dipped in the fondue.

Serves 6

Main Courses

*T*his dish is an exciting variation on plaki, the Greek
method of baking fish in red wine with tomatoes and herbs.

Grecian-style cod

4 cod steaks
30ml/2 tablespoons lemon juice
30ml/2 tablespoons olive oil
3 shallots, or 1 small onion, chopped
1 small bulb fennel, sliced
2 cloves garlic, crushed
10ml/2 teaspoons tomato purée
450g/1lb tomatoes, skinned and chopped
5ml/1 teaspoon chopped thyme
small sprig of rosemary
pinch of cinnamon
60ml/4 tablespoons red wine
salt and freshly ground black pepper
Garnish
black olives
dill

Wash the fish steaks, sprinkle them with lemon juice and set aside. Heat the oil in a pan, then gently cook the shallots, fennel and garlic until tender and golden. Stir in the tomato purée, tomatoes, herbs, cinnamon and wine. Season with salt and pepper, and simmer for 5 minutes. Place the fish in an ovenproof dish and spoon over the sauce. Bake in a pre-heated oven at 180°C/350°F/gas 4 for 20–25 minutes.

Serve garnished with the black·olives and dill, and accompanied by a Greek salad.

This delicate fish mould decorated with succulent prawns makes an impressive dinner party dish.

Scandinavian fish mould

450g/1lb prawns in their shells
750g/1½lb plaice fillets, skinned
2 eggs, separated
5ml/1 teaspoon anchovy essence
150ml/¼ pint single cream
150ml/¼ pint thick natural yoghurt
30ml/2 tablespoons chopped parsley
salt and white pepper
Sauce
450ml/¾ pint water
150ml/¼ pint dry white wine
25g/1oz butter
25g/1oz wholemeal flour
60ml/4 tablespoons single cream
5ml/1 teaspoon tomato purée

Butter a 900ml/1½ pint ring mould. Peel the prawns, reserving the shells, and arrange some in the mould. Put the others aside.

Work the plaice, egg yolks, anchovy essence, cream and yoghurt in a food processor until almost smooth. Stir in the parsley and season. Whisk the egg whites until stiff, and fold into the mixture. Spoon into the mould.

Stand the mould in a roasting tin with enough water to come halfway up the sides. Cover with buttered grease-proof paper and cook at 180°C/350°F/gas 4 for 45 minutes or until set.

Simmer the prawn shells with the water and wine for 25 minutes. Liquidize and sieve. Melt the butter and stir in the flour. Cook for 1 minute, then blend in the liquid from the shells. Stir over a low heat until thickened, then simmer for 5 minutes. Whisk in the cream and tomato purée, season and simmer for 2–3 minutes.

Turn out the mould, fill the centre with the reserved prawns and serve with the sauce, garnished with fresh dill if available.

Serves 6

*Light and creamy, quenelles make an elegant
dish served in a subtly flavoured tarragon sauce.*

Salmon and scallop quenelles

625g/1¼lb tail piece salmon
225g/8oz scallops
salt and white pepper
pinch of nutmeg
150ml/¼ pint double cream
1 egg
1 egg white
Sauce
15g/½oz butter
1 shallot or button onion, finely chopped
150ml/¼ pint fish stock
90ml/6 tablespoons dry white wine
5ml/1 teaspoon chopped tarragon
10ml/2 teaspoons cornflour

Cut the tail piece of salmon horizontally and remove the bone; then cut the fish away from the skin. Separate the corals from the scallops and reserve. Blend together the salmon flesh and white part of the scallops in a food processor until very finely chopped. Add the seasonings, cream, egg and egg white, and process again for 30 seconds until thick. Chill for at least 1 hour.

Melt the butter in a saucepan and cook the shallot until soft. Add the scallop corals and cook over a gentle heat for 5 minutes. Pour in the stock and wine, add the tarragon and seasoning, and simmer for 5 minutes. Purée the sauce in a blender until smooth, then return to the saucepan. Blend the cornflour with a little water, stir into the sauce, and heat gently until thickened.

To cook the quenelles, bring a pan of salted water to the boil, then reduce the heat to simmer. Slide in tablespoonfuls of the fish mixture, a few at a time. Cook very gently for 5 minutes until they are set and cooked through. Remove with a slotted spoon and keep warm while cooking the rest of the mixture.

Serve with the sauce, garnished with sprigs of tarragon.

*S*ole rolls, served in a golden sauce and garnished with vegetables, give this dish that special 'nouvelle' finish.

Sole in saffron sauce

6 medium-size sole fillets, skinned and cut in half
175g/6oz peeled prawns
1 small onion, finely chopped
150ml/¼ pint dry white wine
1 bay leaf
150ml/¼ pint fish stock
large pinch of saffron threads
15g/½oz butter
30ml/2 tablespoons wholemeal flour
100g/4oz fromage frais (low-fat soft cheese)
salt and white pepper
Garnish
100g/4oz thin asparagus, trimmed to leave 5cm/2in tips
2 broccoli spears, divided into tiny florets
1 tomato, skinned, seeded and cut in neat pieces
dill

With the skin side up, place a few prawns at the wide end of each sole fillet. Roll up, secure with a cocktail stick (any remaining prawns can be used for garnishing), and place in an ovenproof dish. Scatter over the onion, pour in the wine, then add the bay leaf and seasoning and cover with buttered foil. Bake at 180°C/350°F/gas 4 for 15–20 minutes until cooked.

Bring the fish stock to the boil and pour over the saffron threads. Allow to infuse for 5–10 minutes, then strain. Melt the butter in a saucepan and blend in the flour. Cook for 1 minute, then gradually add the stock.

Bring a pan of water to the boil, then drop in the asparagus and broccoli and simmer for 2 minutes. Drain, set aside and keep warm.

Carefully remove the sole rolls from the dish and place on serving plates. Strain the liquor and add to the sauce. Bring to the boil, simmer for 2–3 minutes, then whisk in the fromage frais. Season the sauce and pour around the sole rolls. Garnish with the prepared vegetables, finishing with dill.

Exotic fish parcels unfold to reveal exquisite Oriental-style trout cooked with ginger.

Oriental trout parcels

4 medium-size trout, cleaned, fins removed
bunch spring onions, cut into fine shreds
45ml/3 tablespoons ginger, cut into fine threads
juice of 1 lime
45ml/3 tablespoons sesame oil
45ml/3 tablespoons soy sauce
Garnish
spring onion tassels

Prepare four pieces of greaseproof paper to wrap each fish by brushing with a little of the sesame oil. Mix the spring onion and ginger together and use half of it to fill the four fish cavities. Place each fish on the paper, sprinkle over a little lime juice, and some more onion and ginger. Wrap each fish to make a parcel, then steam for 20 minutes in a fish kettle, or on a plate standing in a large casserole.

To serve, carefully unwrap each fish and slide on to a serving plate. Heat the remaining sesame oil and soy sauce in a small saucepan. Bring to simmer, then quickly pour over the fish and serve at once, garnished with spring onion tassels.

This sumptuous fish terrine looks impressive and tastes exquisite but is extremely easy to prepare.

Striped fish terrine

625g/1¼lb cod fillet, skinned
40g/1½oz fresh wheatmeal breadcrumbs
grated rind of ½ lemon
150g/5oz Greek strained yoghurt
2 eggs, separated
15ml/1 tablespoon chopped parsley
salt and white pepper
225g/8oz salmon, skinned
Sauce
15ml/1 tablespoon sunflower oil
1 small onion, finely chopped
450g/1lb tomatoes, skinned and chopped
pinch of sugar

Put the cod into a food processor and blend until finely chopped. Add the breadcrumbs, lemon rind, yoghurt, egg yolks and parsley. Season, then mix again. Whisk the egg whites until stiff and fold into the fish mixture. Spoon half into a buttered terrine or loaf tin. Cut the salmon into small pieces and place in an even layer on top of the white fish mixture; spoon over the remaining mixture. Cover with a piece of buttered greaseproof paper and place in a roasting tin. Pour in enough water to come halfway up the sides of the dish, then cook at 180°C/350°F/gas 4 for about 35–40 minutes, or until firm to the touch.

Heat the oil in a saucepan, then add the onion and cook until soft. Add the tomatoes with seasoning and a pinch of sugar, then simmer for 15 minutes. Press through a sieve to make a sauce, which can be re-heated before serving if you are eating the terrine hot.

Served in a thick, piquant sauce, this is an authentic Mediterranean fish dish, a real favourite in France and Italy.

Mediterranean-style red mullet

4 medium-size red mullet, scales removed
5ml/1 teaspoon olive oil
1 onion, chopped
1 clove garlic, crushed
450g/1lb tomatoes, chopped
1 bay leaf
salt and freshly ground black pepper
150ml/¼ pint red wine
10ml/2 teaspoons chopped oregano
Garnish
oregano

Clean the mullet, leaving the liver intact. Place in an ovenproof dish brushed with oil. Add the onion, garlic, tomatoes, bay leaf and seasoning, then pour over the wine and scatter over the oregano. Cover with foil and bake in a pre-heated oven at 200°C/400°F/gas 6 for 25 minutes, until the mullet are cooked.

Remove, arrange in a serving dish and keep warm. Put the cooking liquid and vegetables into a pan and simmer for 5 minutes. Press through a sieve to give a thick sauce, then pour over the mullet. Garnish with oregano.

Sesame beef sauté

450g/1lb rump steak
30ml/2 tablespoons sunflower oil
225g/8oz button mushrooms, sliced
30ml/2 tablespoons sesame seeds
Marinade
10ml/2 teaspoons sesame oil
10ml/2 teaspoons brown sugar
75ml/5 tablespoons soy sauce
60ml/4 tablespoons dry sherry
1 clove garlic, crushed
2.5ml/½ teaspoon dry ginger
Garnish
4 spring onions, shredded

Cut the steak into very thin slices. Mix the ingredients for the marinade together in a bowl, then add the strips of beef, turning them so that they are all coated with the marinade. Cover and leave to stand for 1 hour.

Drain the meat from the marinade. Heat the oil in a large frying pan or wok, add the meat and cook over a high heat for 3–4 minutes. Stir in the mushrooms and sesame seeds and continue to cook for 3 minutes or until the mushrooms are just tender.

Serve at once, garnished with shreds of spring onion.

Spiced braised steak with chick peas

1 onion, chopped
1 clove garlic, crushed
30ml/2 tablespoons sunflower oil
450g/1lb braising steak, diced
5ml/1 teaspoon ground cumin
2.5ml/½ teaspoon ground ginger
1.25ml/¼ teaspoon ground coriander seeds
1 cardamom, crushed
150ml/¼ pint beef stock
100g/4oz chick peas, soaked overnight
125ml/4floz red wine
salt and freshly ground black pepper
50g/2oz dates, stoned

Cook the onion and garlic in the oil until soft. Add the steak and spices (using only the seeds of the crushed cardamom) and lightly brown. Transfer to an ovenproof casserole and add the beef stock, the drained chick peas, wine and seasoning. Cook in a pre-heated oven at 170°C/325°F/gas 3 for about 2½ hours. Add the dates and cook for a further 30 minutes.

Serve hot with couscous.

Slices of calves liver, sautéed with avocado, apricots and Marsala, create an unusual yet appetizing combination.

Calves liver with apricots and avocado

8 thin slices calves liver
45ml/3 tablespoons wholemeal flour
30ml/2 tablespoons chopped sage
30ml/2 tablespoons golden olive oil
1 shallot, finely chopped
2 large, or 4 medium, apricots, stoned and quartered
1 avocado, peeled and sliced
90ml/6 tablespoons Marsala
salt and freshly ground black pepper
Garnish
sage leaves

Wash the liver and remove the fine membrane from around the edge. Mix together the flour and sage, and season with salt and pepper. Use this mixture to coat each side of the liver. Heat the oil in a large frying pan and add the slices of liver with the shallot. Cook for about 2 minutes each side, then remove and keep warm. Put the apricots and avocado into the pan and cook gently for 2 minutes; remove the avocado and put it with the liver. Pour the Marsala into the pan and bring to the boil. Allow to simmer until it reduces slightly, seasoning if necessary.

Arrange the liver on serving plates with the avocado and apricots, then pour over the sauce. Garnish with sage leaves.

This colourful Mexican dish combines tender meat with tropical fruit and spices to make an exotic main course.

Picadillo de la baja

450g/1lb braising steak, cubed
225g/8oz pork fillet, cubed
30ml/2 tablespoons corn oil
1 onion, chopped
1 clove garlic, crushed
1 hot chilli pepper, seeded and chopped
4 tomatoes, skinned and chopped
pinch each of ground cloves and cinnamon
2.5ml/½ teaspoon paprika
½ red pepper, seeded and chopped
½ green pepper, seeded and chopped
30ml/2 tablespoons raisins
175g/6oz pineapple cubes (fresh or canned in natural juice)
1 mango, peeled and chopped
salt and freshly ground black pepper

Heat the oil in a large frying pan, add the cubed meats and cook until lightly browned. Add the onion, garlic, and chilli and cook until the onion softens. Stir in the tomatoes, spices and 150ml/5floz water. Cover the pan and allow to simmer gently for 45 minutes, adding more water if the casserole becomes too dry. Add the peppers and cook for a further 10 minutes. Stir in the fruit and season if necessary, then cook over a gentle heat for 10 minutes, by which time the tomatoes will have formed a thick sauce.

Serve with boiled brown rice.

61

Mildly hot and aromatic, this lamb curry is served in a creamy yoghurt sauce, garnished with fresh coriander leaves.

Nepalese lamb

625g/1¼lb boneless lean lamb, cubed
45ml/3 tablespoons sunflower oil
1 large onion, sliced
1 clove garlic, crushed
2 dried red chillies, seeded and finely chopped
10ml/2 teaspoons ground cumin
15ml/3 teaspoons ground coriander
2.5ml/½ teaspoon turmeric
2.5ml/½ teaspoon ground ginger
1 cinnamon stick
150ml/¼ pint natural yoghurt
30ml/2 tablespoons lime juice
salt and freshly ground black pepper
50g/2oz cashew nuts, lightly toasted
Garnish
coriander leaves

Heat the oil in a large saucepan. Add the meat and cook until lightly browned, then remove from the pan. Place the onion in the pan and cook for 4–5 minutes over a medium heat until lightly browned. Add the garlic and chillies with the spices and cinnamon stick, then cook for 1 minute. Stir in 150ml/¼ pint water, the yoghurt and the lime juice. Season, and bring to the boil. Replace the meat, cover the pan tightly, and simmer for 1 hour or until the lamb is tender.

Serve scattered with toasted cashew nuts, garnished with coriander leaves, and accompanied with boiled basmati rice.

Cubes of marinated lamb are cooked on skewers and served with a pilaff flavoured with dried fruits and nuts.

Persian lamb kebabs

750g/1½lb boned leg of lamb, cubed
30ml/2 tablespoons olive oil
juice of 1 lemon
pinch each of ground cumin and cinnamon
5ml/1 teaspoon dried oregano
salt and freshly ground black pepper
8 button onions
8 button mushrooms
8 cherry tomatoes
8 bay leaves
Pilaff
50g/2oz dried apricots
15ml/1 tablespoon olive oil
1 small onion, chopped
175g/6oz long-grain brown rice
450ml/¾ pint weak chicken stock
50g/2oz raisins or sultanas
25g/1oz walnuts, roughly chopped

Mix together the olive oil, lemon juice, cumin, cinnamon and oregano, and season. Add the cubes of lamb and allow to marinate for at least 2–4 hours, or overnight. In the meantime, pour boiling water over the apricots and leave to soak.

Thread the lamb on to 8 small wooden skewers or 4 long kebab skewers with the onions, mushrooms, tomatoes and bay leaves. Set aside.

Drain and chop the apricots. Heat the oil in a medium-size saucepan and gently cook the onion until soft. Stir in the rice and cook for 1 minute, coating each grain with the oil. Pour in the stock, add the apricots and simmer for 25 minutes until the rice is cooked and all the water absorbed. Stir in the raisins and walnuts and season if necessary.

Place the kebabs under a hot grill, turning them as they cook and brushing them with the marinade to keep them moist. Serve with pilaff rice.

Inspired by the traditional Greek spinach pie, this appetizing strudel contains fresh spinach, cabbage and feta cheese.

Vegetable strudel

15ml/1 tablespoon sunflower oil
1 medium-size onion, chopped
1 clove garlic, crushed
225g/8oz white cabbage, shredded
1kg/2lb spinach, washed and shredded
2.5ml/½ teaspoon cinnamon
15ml/1 tablespoon chopped fresh oregano
225g/8oz feta cheese, crumbled
25g/1oz freshly grated Parmesan cheese
1 egg, beaten
salt and freshly ground black pepper
225g/8oz filo pastry
25g/1oz butter, melted
sesame seeds
Garnish
onion rings
black olives

Heat the oil in a very large saucepan, add the onion and garlic and cook gently for a few minutes until soft. Add the cabbage and spinach and cook, turning until the cabbage and spinach soften. Allow to cool and drain off the liquid. Add the cinnamon, oregano, cheeses and egg, and season.

Lay the filo pastry on a flat surface and spread over the filling. Roll up from the longest side, stopping at each turn to brush the pastry with melted butter. Transfer to a greased baking sheet, bending the roll to fit in the tray. Brush the top with butter and sprinkle with sesame seeds. Bake at 200°C/400 °F/gas 6 for 25 minutes or until crisp and golden.

Serve sliced, garnished with onion rings and black olives.

Serves 6

Vegetable couscous

75g/3oz chick peas, soaked overnight
225g/8oz couscous
15ml/1 tablespoon sunflower oil
1 onion, sliced
1 clove garlic, chopped
2 carrots, sliced
2 leeks, trimmed and chopped
2.5ml/½ teaspoon each of cumin, coriander and cinnamon
600ml/1 pint vegetable stock
15ml/1 tablespoon tomato purée
1 green pepper, seeded and diced
2 tomatoes, skinned and chopped
2 courgettes, sliced
100g/4oz French beans
salt and freshly ground black pepper

Drain the chick peas and simmer for 45 minutes. Soak the couscous in 450ml/¾ pint water for 10–15 minutes.

Heat the oil in a large saucepan, add the onion and garlic, and cook gently for 5 minutes. Add the chick peas, carrots, leeks and spices, then pour in the stock and tomato purée. Bring to the boil, then reduce the heat to simmer.

Line a large sieve, or the upper half of a steamer, with muslin. Put in the couscous and place over the simmering vegetables. Cover with foil and cook for 20 minutes. Add the green pepper, tomatoes, courgettes and French beans to the stew. Replace the couscous, fluffing it up with a fork, and continue to cook for 10 minutes. Season the vegetables if necessary.

Make a border of couscous on a serving dish, then spoon the vegetables into the middle.

Rice and onion flan

225g/8oz cooked brown rice
75g/3oz Cheddar cheese, finely grated
1 egg, beaten
Filling
30ml/2 tablespoons sunflower oil
2 medium-size onions, thinly sliced
6 spring onions, chopped
45ml/3 tablespoons semi-skimmed milk
2 eggs
salt and freshly ground black pepper
pinch of cayenne

Grease a 20cm/8in flan tin. Mix together the rice, cheese and egg, and season with salt and pepper. Press the mixture into the flan tin, covering the base and sides evenly. Cook in the oven at 190°C/375°F/gas 5 for 15 minutes.

Meanwhile, heat the oil in a pan and cook the sliced onions slowly for 10 minutes or until they are soft. Drain off the oil and spoon into the flan case with the chopped spring onion. Beat the milk and eggs together, season, then pour over the onions. Bake in the oven for 25 minutes or until the filling is set and golden.

To remove the flan from the tin, ease it away from the rim with the point of a knife and serve while warm.

*P*lump chicken breasts are stuffed with rice and ham and flavoured with garlic for an authentic Italian dish.

Italian stuffed chicken

4 boneless chicken breasts, skinned
25g/1oz cooked ham, diced
50g/2oz cooked brown rice
1 clove garlic, crushed
15ml/1 tablespoon chopped parsley
½ egg, beaten
salt and freshly ground black pepper
30ml/2 tablespoons olive oil
150ml/¼ pint chicken stock
60ml/4 tablespoons dry white wine
30ml/2 tablespoons tomato purée
Garnish
cooked pasta
parsley

Cut through the chicken breasts horizontally to make a pocket and season inside. Mix together the ham, rice, garlic and parsley, and stir in the egg to bind. Season with salt and pepper. Divide between the four chicken breasts, then secure the opening with cocktail sticks.

Heat the oil in a frying pan, add the chicken breasts, and sauté on each side until golden. Drain off any excess oil. Combine the stock, wine and tomato purée, and pour over the chicken. Cover and simmer for 30 minutes, or until the chicken is tender.

Remove the chicken and boil the sauce to reduce and thicken it. Pour over the chicken. Serve garnished with a little cooked pasta and parsley, accompanied with green beans.

*Strips of chicken and crunchy vegetables are
stir-fried in a spicy sauce for a quick, tasty meal.*

Oriental chicken

3 chicken breasts, boned and skinned
30ml/2 tablespoons sunflower oil
1 clove garlic, crushed
225g/8oz broccoli, cut into florets
4 spring onions, chopped
1 green pepper, seeded and sliced
1 red pepper, seeded and sliced
1 yellow pepper, seeded and sliced
30ml/2 tablespoons soy sauce
10ml/2 teaspoons chilli sauce

Cut the chicken into strips. Heat the oil in a wok or large frying pan, then add the chicken and cook over a high heat until lightly browned. Add the garlic and all the vegetables and stir-fry for 3–4 minutes until tender but crisp. Stir in the soy sauce and chilli sauce and heat through.

Serve immediately.

Ideal for summer lunches and picnics, this colourful roulade is enlivened by a fresh yoghurt and dill sauce.

Chicken and broccoli roulade

25g/1oz butter
1 small onion, chopped
100g/4oz mushrooms, chopped
225g/8oz fromage frais (low-fat soft cheese)
225g/8oz cooked chicken, diced
pinch of nutmeg
350g/12oz broccoli
4 eggs, separated
30ml/2 tablespoons freshly grated Parmesan
salt and freshly ground black pepper
Sauce
60ml/4 tablespoons mayonnaise
60ml/4 tablespoons natural yoghurt
15ml/1 tablespoon chopped dill

Heat the butter in a pan, then add the onion and cook until soft. Add the mushrooms and cook for 2 minutes. Allow to cool. Stir in the fromage frais and chicken, and season with nutmeg, salt and pepper.

Grease and line a 28cm/11in Swiss roll tin with greaseproof paper. Heat the oven to 190°C/375°F/gas 5. Trim the broccoli and cook in a little water for a few minutes until just tender. Drain well, then put into a food processor with the egg yolks and chop finely. Whisk the egg whites until stiff, then fold into the broccoli mixture with the grated Parmesan. Pour into the tin and cook for 20–25 minutes. Allow to cool slightly before turning on to a fresh piece of greaseproof paper. Remove the lining paper carefully, trim the edges and roll up from the long side. When cold, unroll and spread the filling over. Roll up again and place on a serving plate.

Mix together the ingredients for the sauce and serve with slices of roulade, garnished with extra dill.

The essence of Indonesian cuisine: marinated chicken cooked on skewers is served with a spicy nut sauce.

Chicken satay

450g/1lb boneless chicken breasts, skinned
1 small onion, chopped
1 clove garlic, crushed
30ml/2 tablespoons light soy sauce
2.5ml/½ teaspoon each of ground ginger and coriander
15ml/1 tablespoon lemon juice
10ml/2 teaspoons oil
salt and pepper
Sauce
75g/3oz desiccated coconut
15ml/1 tablespoon oil
1 small onion, finely chopped
1 clove garlic, crushed
45ml/3 tablespoons peanut butter
2.5ml/½ teaspoon chilli sauce
5ml/1 teaspoon brown sugar
Garnish
cucumber slices
shredded spring onion

Cut the chicken into 2.5cm/1in cubes and put into a bowl. Mix together the onion, garlic, soy sauce, spices and lemon juice. Season, then add to the chicken and leave for at least 2 hours. Put the desiccated coconut into a bowl, pour over 300ml/½ pint boiling water and allow to stand.

Thread the chicken on to bamboo skewers, brush with a little oil and cook under a hot grill for 6–8 minutes until golden brown and tender, turning them during cooking.

Cook the onion and garlic in the oil until soft. Add the peanut butter, chilli sauce and brown sugar. Strain the coconut, add the liquid to the sauce, and heat through, mixing thoroughly to give a smooth consistency.

Serve with the cooked chicken, and garnish with cucumber slices and shredded spring onion.

The texture of tender turkey escalopes is enhanced by a tangy sauce for a really imaginative main course.

Citrus turkey escalopes

8 small slices of turkey breast
1 orange
15g/½oz butter
30ml/2 tablespoons olive oil
grated rind and juice of 1 lime
5ml/1 teaspoon grated ginger
150ml/¼ pint chicken stock
2.5ml/½ teaspoon cornflour
salt and freshly ground black pepper
Garnish
lime slices

Place the escalopes between cling film and beat out until quite thin. Peel the orange and cut the skin into fine shreds, or use a zester to cut orange strips. Remove all the pith from the orange and cut into slices.

Heat the butter and oil in a frying pan and cook the turkey slices for 8 minutes, turning them once. Remove from the pan and keep warm. Put the orange shreds and slices into the pan and cook for 1 minute to heat through, then put to one side with the turkey.

Add the lime juice and rind to the pan with the ginger and stock, and boil to reduce a little. Blend the cornflour with a little water, add to the sauce and simmer to thicken. Season if necessary.

Serve with the orange slices, pour over the sauce, and garnish with lime slices.

*T*urkey roll studded with bright, crisp vegetables and served with Marsala sauce makes a delightful dish.

Jewelled turkey roll

750g/1½lb turkey breast slices
100g/4oz wholemeal breadcrumbs
1 bunch watercress, trimmed and finely chopped
1 clove garlic, crushed
salt and freshly ground black pepper
1 egg, beaten
100g/4oz carrots, cut into thin sticks, blanched 4 minutes
100g/4oz courgettes, cut into thin strips, blanched 2 minutes
75g/3oz fine green beans, trimmed, blanched 3 minutes
1 red pepper, seeded and cut into strips
8 button mushrooms, halved
150ml/¼ pint dry white wine
Sauce
5ml/1 teaspoon sunflower margarine
15ml/1 tablespoon wholemeal flour
210ml/7floz chicken stock
45ml/3 tablespoons Marsala

Place a slice of turkey between cling film and beat out until thin and almost twice its size. Set aside and repeat with the rest. Lay out on a flat surface so that the slices overlap each other to form a rectangle about 38cm/15in by 25cm/10in. Season.

Mix together the breadcrumbs, watercress and garlic, then season and bind together with the egg. Spread over the turkey. Arrange the vegetables in alternate rows, and then carefully roll up. Using thin string, tie the roll at intervals, then cut in half. Put the two rolls into an ovenproof dish and pour over the wine. Cover and cook at 190°C/375°F/gas 5 for 45 minutes. Lift out the rolls, remove the string and keep warm.

Melt the margarine in a saucepan, stir in the flour and cook for 1 minute. Add the stock and the juice from the turkey, then bring to the boil and simmer for 2 minutes. Add the Marsala and cook for a further 2 minutes.

Slice the turkey and serve with the sauce and garnished with sprigs of watercress.

Serves 6

Duck with kumquats

4 duck breasts, boned and skinned
10ml/2 teaspoons salted black beans
30ml/2 tablespoons sunflower oil
1 clove garlic, finely chopped
4 slices ginger, shredded
100g/4oz kumquats, sliced and pips removed
125ml/4floz chicken stock
45ml/3 tablespoons soy sauce
15ml/1 tablespoon Chinese red vinegar
Garnish
3 spring onions, finely chopped

Cut the duck into thin slices and set aside. Put the black beans into a bowl of water and leave to soak for 10 minutes, then drain.

Heat the oil in a large frying pan or wok, then add the beans and garlic and cook for 2 minutes. Stir in the duck and ginger and cook for 3 minutes, turning the ingredients all the time. Add the rest of the ingredients and allow to cook for 2 minutes.

Serve immediately sprinkled with chopped spring onion.

Salads & Vegetables

This Middle Eastern dish of broad beans and rice is dressed with yoghurt and served on a bed of spinach.

Broad bean and rice salad

450g/1lb shelled broad beans, fresh or frozen
225g/8oz cooked long-grain brown rice
few well-washed spinach leaves
Dressing
150ml/¼ pint yoghurt
1 clove garlic, crushed
pinch of paprika
25g/1oz pine nuts
salt and freshly ground black pepper
Garnish
few chopped chives

Boil the beans in unsalted water until tender (salt will harden them), and drain. Remove the skins and mix with the rice. Mix together all the ingredients for the dressing and stir into the rice.

Chill before serving on a bed of spinach and sprinkled with chopped chives.

A lively mix of textures and flavours, this Chinese salad is the perfect accompaniment for any Oriental meal.

Chinese salad

½ head Chinese leaves
75g/3oz spinach, shredded
100g/4oz baby sweetcorn, cooked
5cm/2in piece cucumber, cut into sticks
5 spring onions, shredded
sesame seeds
Dressing
45ml/3 tablespoons sunflower oil
30ml/2 tablespoons light soy sauce
pinch of chilli powder

Shred the Chinese leaves and put them into a salad bowl with the spinach. Halve the baby sweetcorn and add to the salad with the cucumber sticks and spring onions. Mix together the ingredients for the dressing, then pour over the salad and toss.

Sprinkle with sesame seeds and serve.

Crunchy cauliflower florets and apple chunks in a curried dressing are ideal served with cold chicken and turkey.

Curried cauliflower salad

1 cauliflower, divided into small florets
2 medium-size dessert apples, cored and diced
2 carrots, grated
50g/2oz sultanas or raisins
50g/2oz walnuts, coarsely chopped
Dressing
45ml/3 tablespoons low-calorie mayonnaise
60ml/4 tablespoons natural yoghurt
5ml/1 teaspoon curry paste
15ml/1 tablespoon lemon juice

Bring a saucepan of water to the boil, then add the cauliflower and simmer for 2 minutes. Drain and refresh under cold water, then put into a salad bowl with the diced apple, carrots and sultanas.

Mix together the ingredients for the dressing, pour over the salad and toss together. Just before serving add the chopped walnuts.

T his fresh salad uses unusual varieties of lettuce, and combines creamy avocado with the sharp taste of oranges.

Avocado and citrus salad

2 varieties of lettuce, e.g. frisée, red leaved variety,
little gem
2 medium-size oranges, peeled and segmented
1 grapefruit, peeled, segmented and halved
1 large avocado, halved, peeled and sliced
15ml/1 tablespoon sunflower seeds
Dressing
rind and juice of 1 lime
30ml/2 tablespoons sunflower oil
30ml/2 tablespoons olive oil
5ml/1 teaspoon clear honey
salt and freshly ground black pepper

Wash and dry the lettuce and arrange in a bowl with the orange and grapefruit segments and slices of avocado. Mix together the ingredients for the dressing, then pour over the salad.

Sprinkle over the sunflower seeds and serve.

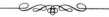

Lentil and tomato salad

225g/8oz brown Continental lentils
1 small onion, chopped
2 spring onions or shallots, chopped
3 tomatoes, quartered
75ml/5 tablespoons olive oil
10ml/2 teaspoons white wine vinegar (optional)
salt and freshly ground black pepper
30ml/2 tablespoons chopped parsley and mint

Soak the lentils for about 1 hour and remove any gritty pieces. Drain and cook in fresh water for about 1¼ hours, or until tender. Strain and mix with the chopped onion and tomatoes. Mix the olive oil with the vinegar, if used, and season. Toss the lentil salad in the dressing and sprinkle with parsley and mint.

Serve with crusty brown bread and hard-boiled eggs.

Bulgur wheat pilaff

25g/1oz butter
15ml/1 tablespoon sunflower oil
1 medium-size onion, finely chopped
225g/8oz bulgur wheat
450ml/¾ pint boiling chicken stock
2 tomatoes, skinned and chopped
50g/2oz seedless raisins
2.5ml/½ teaspoon ground cumin
2.5ml/½ teaspoon ground coriander
salt and freshly ground black pepper

Heat the butter and oil together in a large saucepan. Add the onion and, stirring all the time, cook until golden brown. Stir in the bulgur wheat so that all the grains are coated in the oil, then pour in the stock and boil for 5 minutes. Reduce the heat, cover and cook for 20 minutes, by which time most of the liquid will have been absorbed.

Add the tomatoes, raisins and spices. Season and cook for 5 minutes. Stir the pilaff well, then serve hot.

This bean casserole is cooked with tomatoes and honey and lightly spiced with cloves and coriander.

Greek bean casserole

50g/2oz black-eyed beans
50g/2oz butter beans
50g/2oz red kidney beans
50g/2oz borlotti beans
75g/3oz flageolet beans
1 onion, chopped
1 clove garlic, crushed
45ml/3 tablespoons tomato paste
300ml/½ pint water
2 tomatoes, skinned and sliced
pinch each of ground cloves and coriander
15ml/1 tablespoon wine vinegar
10ml/2 teaspoons honey
salt and freshly ground black pepper

Soak all the beans overnight. Drain. Place the red kidney beans in a pan with fresh water, and boil for 10 minutes. Drain and refresh under running water. Put into the saucepan with the rest of the beans and cook in boiling water for about 1 hour, or until just tender.

Cook the onion and garlic in the oil until soft and translucent. Stir in the tomato paste and then the water, sliced tomato and spices.

Cook for 2 minutes, add the vinegar and honey, and season to taste. Stir in the beans and transfer to an ovenproof casserole dish. Cover with a lid and cook in a pre-heated oven at 170°C/325°F/gas 3 for 30 minutes.

Serve hot.

*With a mildly curry-flavoured dressing, this tasty
dish is ideal as a light meal or a spicy side salad.*

Spicy tuna and pasta salad

175g/6oz wholemeal pasta shells
200g/7oz can tuna in brine, drained
90ml/6 tablespoons reduced-calorie mayonnaise
2.5ml/½ teaspoon curry paste
salt and freshly ground black pepper
juice of ½ lemon
4 spring onions, chopped
Garnish
chopped parsley

Cook the pasta shells in boiling salted water until tender, then drain and cool. Break the tuna up into flakes and mix with the pasta.

Blend the mayonnaise with the curry paste, seasoning and lemon juice, then pour over the salad. Add the spring onions and toss together.

Pile the salad into a serving dish and scatter over the chopped parsley.

*T his simple stir-fry dish makes a quick, spicy
alternative to traditional-style vegetables.*

Stir-fried vegetables with tofu

15ml/1 tablespoon sunflower oil
2 large carrots, thinly sliced
1 large clove garlic, finely chopped
225g/8oz pak choi leaves, shredded
100g/4oz mushrooms, sliced
1 large leek, shredded
2.5ml/½ teaspoon Chinese curry powder
30ml/2 tablespoons light soy sauce
225g/8oz tofu, drained and cubed

Heat the oil in a large frying pan or wok, then add the carrots and garlic and cook for 3 minutes. Stir in the pak choi, mushrooms and leek, and cook for a further 2 minutes. Add the spice, soy sauce and tofu, and stir-fry for 1–2 minutes to heat up the tofu.

Serve immediately.

The flavours and textures of leeks and carrots combine perfectly to produce this unusual vegetable dish.

Carrot and leek timbales

625g/1¼lb carrots, chopped
25g/1oz butter
450g/1lb leeks, trimmed and finely chopped
1 egg, beaten
salt and freshly ground black pepper

Cook the carrots in a little water until tender, then drain and chop very finely in a blender or food processor.

Melt the butter in a saucepan, add the leeks and gently sweat until the leeks soften. Stir in the carrots, seasoning and egg. Spoon the mixture into 6 greased dariole moulds, then place them in a roasting dish with water coming halfway up the sides of the moulds. Cover the dishes with a piece of buttered greaseproof paper and cook in a pre-heated oven at 190°C/375°F/gas 5 for 45 minutes or until set.

Turn out on to a serving plate and serve as an accompaniment to a main course.

Chicory and hazelnut salad

350g/12oz chicory, sliced
1 small head radicchio, finely shredded
100g/4oz lambs lettuce
50g/2oz hazelnuts, toasted, roughly chopped
Dressing
30ml/2 tablespoons hazelnut oil
15ml/1 tablespoon sunflower oil
2.5ml/½ teaspoon Dijon mustard
pinch of sugar
salt and freshly ground black pepper

Mix together the ingredients for the dressing in a large bowl. Add the chicory and radicchio and toss together. Line a salad bowl with the lambs lettuce, pile in the chicory and radicchio, then sprinkle over the chopped hazelnuts.

Celeriac and carrot salad

350g/12oz celeriac, scrubbed
30ml/2 tablespoons white wine vinegar
2 large carrots
3 spring onions, shredded
30ml/2 tablespoons sunflower oil
5ml/1 teaspoon caraway seeds
salt and freshly ground black pepper

Peel the celeriac and cut into very fine sticks that resemble shreds. Put in a bowl, sprinkle with vinegar and toss to coat thoroughly. Cut the carrot in the same way and add to the celeriac with the spring onion. Pour over the oil, add the caraway seeds, then season and toss together. Cover and refrigerate for 1 hour before serving.

This colourful rice dish is the ideal accompaniment for grilled meats, fish and especially kebabs.

Spanish rice

30ml/2 tablespoons olive oil
½ Spanish onion, chopped
2 cloves garlic, chopped
1 green chilli, seeded and finely chopped
350g/12oz long-grain brown rice
350g/12oz tomatoes, skinned and chopped
good pinch of saffron threads
600ml/1 pint vegetable stock
½ red pepper, seeded and diced
½ green pepper, seeded and diced
100g/4oz fresh or frozen peas
salt and freshly ground black pepper

Put the oil into a large saucepan, add the onion and garlic, and cook until soft and translucent. Add the chilli and rice and cook for 2 minutes. Stir in the tomatoes, saffron and stock, bring to the boil, then simmer for 30 minutes. If the rice becomes dry, add a little water. Stir in the peppers and peas, and cook the rice for a further 10 minutes or until the rice is tender.

Season with salt and pepper and serve hot.

*W*inter vegetables eaten raw in salads capture
the crispness and freshness of summer.

Winter salad

1 small red cabbage, finely shredded
5 sticks celery, sliced
1 green pepper, seeded and sliced
1 yellow pepper, seeded and sliced
½ bunch spring onions, chopped
Dressing
60ml/4 tablespoons sunflower oil
30ml/2 tablespoons cider vinegar
5ml/1 teaspoon grainy mustard
5ml/1 teaspoon clear honey
salt and freshly ground black pepper

Put the shredded cabbage into a bowl with the celery, peppers and spring onions. Mix together the ingredients for the dressing, then pour over the salad and toss together.

Bursting with vitamins and minerals, sprouting beans taste delicious when tossed together in a salad.

Sprouted salad

25g/1oz soya beans
50g/2oz chick peas
50g/2oz aduki beans
50g/2oz mung beans
50g/2oz green lentils
1 red-skinned onion, finely sliced
Dressing
45ml/3 tablespoons sunflower oil
juice of ½ orange
salt and freshly ground black pepper

Put the different beans into separate bowls, cover with water and leave to soak overnight. Drain and put each into large, wide-necked jars. Cover with muslin or cheesecloth, secure with an elastic band and place in a warm, dark place (e.g. an airing cupboard). Twice a day, fill the jars with water, then drain through the muslin to rinse the beans. Repeat for 4–6 days, then remove the beans and rinse before using. Sprouted beans can be stored in the refrigerator in airtight containers for 3–4 days.

To make the salad, mix the beans with the onion and pile into a salad bowl. Mix the dressing and pour over just before serving.

Mushroom risotto

25g/1oz porcini (Italian dried mushrooms)
30ml/2 tablespoons olive oil
1 onion, chopped
225g/8oz long-grain brown rice
450ml/³⁄4 pint hot chicken stock
225g/8oz button mushrooms, quartered
salt and freshly ground black pepper
15g/¹⁄2oz freshly grated Parmesan cheese

Soak the dried mushrooms in 300ml/¼ pint lukewarm water for at least 30 minutes. Strain and reserve the liquid.

Heat the oil in a large saucepan, add the onion and cook gently until soft and translucent. Add the rice and cook for 2–3 minutes. Slowly pour in the stock so that it continually simmers and continue to cook for 10 minutes. Chop the mushrooms and add to the rice with the mushroom liquid. Cook on a low heat for a further 20 minutes.

Season the rice, add the quartered mushrooms and a little water if the risotto becomes dry. Cook for 5 minutes.

Spoon into a serving dish and sprinkle the Parmesan cheese over the top before serving.

Desserts

Jewel-like berries are moulded into delightful heart shapes, making the most of summer's soft fruit harvest.

Berry hearts

350g/12oz blackcurrants, redcurrants, blueberries or bilberries
juice of ½ lemon
15g/½oz gelatine
50g/2oz sugar
300ml/½ pint rosé wine
Decoration
a few extra berries

Put the lemon juice into a measuring jug and make up to 150ml/¼ pint with water. Sprinkle over the gelatine, then leave to soak and become spongy. Put the jug in a pan of simmering water and stir until the gelatine has dissolved. Remove the jug from the pan, and add the sugar, stirring until dissolved, then pour in the wine. Chill the jelly until it begins to thicken. Stir in the fruit and spoon into 6 individual heart-shaped moulds with a capacity of 150ml/¼ pint. Carefully place in the refrigerator and allow to set.

To serve, turn the jellies out on to plates and decorate with the extra berries.

Hazelnut pastry gives an interesting flavour and texture to this classic dessert, decorated with seasonal fruits.

French fruit tart

100g/4oz sunflower margarine
100g/4oz wholemeal flour
75g/3oz plain flour
75g/3oz toasted hazelnuts, very finely chopped
25g/1oz light brown soft sugar
Filling
225g/8oz quark or low-fat soft cheese
30ml/2 tablespoons orange liqueur
100g/4oz green grapes, halved and pips removed
100g/4oz black grapes, halved and pips removed
4 mandarin oranges, peeled and segmented
45ml/3 tablespoons apricot jam

Rub the margarine into the flours. Stir in the chopped hazelnuts and the sugar, then mix to a dough with a little water. Knead lightly, then roll out and use to line a long rectangular loose-bottomed flan tin. Trim the edges and chill for 30 minutes. Prick the base, line with foil and bake at 190°C/375°F/gas 5 for 15 minutes. Remove the foil and cook for 5 minutes more or until golden. Allow to cool.

Beat the quark with the liqueur, spread over the base of the flan and arrange the fruit in rows. Heat the jam gently with 10ml/2 teaspoons water until melted. Sieve and use the glaze to brush over the fruit.

Serve cold.

Bramble mousse is marbled with a swirl of cool yoghurt to give this stunning dessert a truly romantic feel.

Marbled bramble mousse

350g/12oz blackberries, thawed if frozen
30ml/2 tablespoons clear honey
grated rind and juice of ½ lemon
15g/½oz gelatine
2 egg whites
150ml/¼ pint natural yoghurt

Put the blackberries into a saucepan with the honey, lemon rind and juice. Cook over a gentle heat for 5 minutes, then purée in a blender and pour into a bowl to cool.

Put 75ml/5 tablespoons water into a small bowl and sprinkle over the gelatine. Leave to stand until spongy, then place the bowl over a saucepan of simmering water and stir until the gelatine dissolves. Stir into the fruit purée, then chill until the mixture begins to thicken.

Whisk the egg whites until stiff, fold into the fruit mixture, and then pour into a serving bowl. Spoon the yoghurt into the centre of the mousse and, using a large spoon, swirl around to create a marbled effect on the top. Chill for at least 2 hours to allow the mousse to set.

When serving, you will find a pool of yoghurt in the centre.

Pashka

450g/1lb curd cheese
15ml/1 tablespoon honey
2.5ml/½ teaspoon vanilla essence
50g/2oz almonds, chopped
50g/2oz raisins
25g/1oz dried apricots, finely chopped
grated rind of 1 orange
90ml/6 tablespoons natural yoghurt
Decoration
whole blanched almonds
1 kiwi fruit, sliced

Line a 1 litre/1¾ pint basin with a double thickness of scalded muslin. Beat the cheese, honey and vanilla essence together in a bowl until smooth. Stir in the almonds, raisins, apricots, orange rind and yoghurt, then spoon into the basin and fold the cloth over. Cover with a saucer and place a weight on top. Refrigerate overnight.

Remove the weight and saucer. Unfold the cloth, then turn on to a serving plate, peeling away the muslin. Decorate the top with almonds and arrange the slices of kiwi fruit around the bottom.

Orange and grapefruit sorbet

225g/8oz sugar
600ml/1 pint water
1 lemon
2 large grapefruit
4 oranges
2 egg whites

In a saucepan dissolve the sugar in the water. Pare the rinds from the fruit, add to the pan and simmer for 2 minutes. Remove from the heat, cover and leave to stand for 1 hour.

Strain the syrup into a bowl, then squeeze the juice from the fruit and add to the syrup. Pour into a shallow dish and freeze until mushy, i.e. for about 2 hours. Turn into a bowl, whisk and return to the freezer. After 1 hour, remove from the freezer and whisk again. Whisk the egg whites until stiff and fold into the sorbet. Replace in the freezer until firm.

About 1 hour before serving, transfer the sorbet to the refrigerator.

A light sponge, spread with an almond filling and topped with plump, fresh cherries, makes a perfect end to a meal.

Cherry almond flan

2 eggs
50g/2oz light brown soft sugar
50g/2oz wholemeal flour plus 10ml/2 teaspoons flour
Filling
2 egg yolks
25g/1oz caster sugar
15ml/1 tablespoon cornflour
150ml/¼ pint semi-skimmed milk
25g/1oz ground almonds
few drops of almond essence
15ml/1 tablespoon kirsch
225g/8oz dessert cherries, stoned
30ml/2 tablespoons black cherry jam

Grease a 20cm/8in raised-base sponge flan tin and dust with the 10ml/2 teaspoons flour, knocking out any excess. Whisk the eggs and sugar in a bowl until very thick. Carefully fold in the flour, then pour into the tin and bake at 180°C/350°F/gas 4 for 20–25 minutes, until the sponge is light golden brown and springs back when pressed lightly. Turn out and leave to cool.

Whisk the egg yolks and sugar together until pale and light, then whisk in the cornflour. Warm the milk and pour on to the egg mixture. Return to the pan and, stirring all the time, heat until thickened. Beat in the ground almonds and essence and leave to cool.

Sprinkle the kirsch over the sponge, then spread over the cooled custard and arrange the cherries on top. Warm and sieve the jam, then brush over the cherries.

Serve cold.

*Lacy pancakes envelop a luscious filling of
fromage frais and fresh, juicy strawberries.*

Strawberry pancakes

Pancakes
50g/2oz wholemeal flour
50g/2oz plain flour
pinch of salt
2 eggs
300ml/½ pint semi-skimmed milk
Filling
225g/8oz fromage frais (low-fat soft cheese)
25g/1oz sugar
5ml/1 teaspoon orange flower water
225g/8oz strawberries, hulled and sliced

Put the flours and salt into a bowl, add the eggs with a little milk and beat together until smooth. Add the rest of the milk and continue to beat until the batter is smooth and creamy. Leave to stand for 30 minutes.

Butter a small omelette pan. When it sizzles, pour in enough batter to cover the base thinly and evenly. Cook both sides of the pancake until golden brown. Slide on to a warmed plate and repeat until all the batter is used up.

Beat together the fromage frais, sugar and orange flower water. Fold in the strawberries then divide the filling between the warm pancakes. Fold them over to make cornets and serve immediately.

This fabulously light cheesecake sits on a crunchy biscuit base and is laden with fresh, ripe raspberries.

Raspberry cheesecake

50g/2oz butter
100g/4oz digestive biscuits, crushed
350g/12oz curd cheese
2 x 150ml/¼ pint cartons low-fat raspberry yoghurt
50g/2oz caster sugar
juice of ½ lemon
15g/½oz gelatine
3 egg whites
Decoration
225g/8oz raspberries
150ml/¼ pint whipping cream

Melt the butter, stir in the crushed biscuits and turn into the base of a 20cm/8in loose-bottomed spring flan tin. Beat the cheese, yoghurt and sugar until smooth. Pour the lemon juice into a small bowl with 30ml/2 table-spoons water, sprinkle over the gelatine and allow to become spongy. Set the bowl in a saucepan of simmering water and stir to dissolve the gelatine. Cool slightly, whisk into the cheese mixture and refrigerate until it begins to thicken.

Whisk the egg whites until stiff, fold into the mixture, then pour on to the biscuit base. Chill until set.

Remove from the tin and arrange the raspberries on top. Pipe the whipped cream around the raspberries to decorate.

Serves 6–8

Stuffed peaches with walnuts

4 large ripe peaches
40g/1½oz walnuts
100g/4oz macaroons or ratafia biscuits
1 egg yolk
15ml/1 tablespoon brandy
15ml/1 tablespoon yoghurt
175g/6oz raspberries, thawed if frozen

Wash the peaches gently and pat dry with absorbent kitchen paper. Cut each in half and remove the stone. Carefully hollow out a little of the flesh in each to enlarge the cavity, and set aside.

Grind the walnuts and macaroons almost to a powder in a blender and mix with the egg yolk, reserved peach flesh, brandy and the yoghurt. The mixture should have the consistency of a fairly stiff paste. Divide it between the peach halves and sandwich them together so that a little filling is just visible around the centre of each. Sieve the raspberries and sweeten to taste.

Spoon between four plates and then place a stuffed peach on each.

Coconut rice condé

75g/3oz creamed coconut
300ml/½ pint water
600ml/1 pint semi-skimmed milk
100g/4oz short-grain brown rice
10ml/2 teaspoons honey
75ml/5 tablespoons Greek strained yoghurt
freshly grated nutmeg

Put the creamed coconut into a saucepan. Add the water and bring to the boil. Simmer until the coconut dissolves. Add the milk and rice, and continue to simmer for 1 hour or until the rice is tender and the milk is absorbed.

Stir in the honey, then turn into a bowl and allow to cool. Fold in the yoghurt. Spoon into individual glasses and chill until ready to serve.

Before serving, sprinkle the tops with a little grated nutmeg.

*Bursting at the seams, this sumptuous pudding
spills forth its bounty of soft summer fruit.*

Summer pudding

12 slices wholemeal bread, crusts removed
100g/4oz light brown soft sugar
30ml/2 tablespoons port
450g/1lb blackcurrants
225g/8oz redcurrants
225g/8oz raspberries
225g/8oz tayberries, blackberries or loganberries
225g/8oz strawberries, hulled
Decoration
strawberry leaves

Line the base and sides of a 2 litre/3½ pint bowl with bread. Put the sugar and port into a large saucepan with 30ml/2 tablespoons water, then add the blackcurrants and redcurrants and heat gently until the sugar dissolves and the juice has just begun to run from the fruit. Stir in the rest of the fruit and allow to cool. Spoon into the bread-lined bowl, then cover with the rest of the bread and spoon over any remaining fruit juice. Place a piece of greaseproof paper on top followed by a small plate. Put into the refrigerator, place a weight on top of the plate and leave overnight.

To serve, remove the weight, plate and paper and turn the pudding out on to a serving dish. Decorate with strawberry leaves if available.

Serves 8–10

Thin slices of orange and lemon are glazed in a light pastry case for a simple yet tangy dessert.

Citrus tart

75g/3oz butter
75g/3oz plain flour
75g/3oz wholemeal flour
grated rind of 1 lemon
1 egg yolk
Filling
50g/2oz butter
25g/1oz light brown soft sugar
25g/1oz plain flour
1 egg
60ml/4 tablespoons natural yoghurt
450ml/¾ pint fresh orange juice
175g/6oz sugar
2 oranges, thinly sliced
1 lemon, thinly sliced

Rub the butter into the flours and stir in the lemon rind. Add the egg yolk with 15ml/1 tablespoon water to bind the mixture together. Roll out and line a 23cm/9in flan tin.

Beat the butter and brown sugar together until creamy. Beat in the flour, then add the egg and yoghurt and continue to beat until smooth. Pour into the flan case and cook at 200°C/400 °F/gas 6 for 30 minutes.

Simmer the orange juice and sugar in a saucepan until the sugar dissolves. Add the slices of orange and lemon and simmer for 30 minutes until tender. Remove the fruit and boil the juice until it reduces to a syrup. Arrange the orange and lemon slices in the flan, then spoon over the glaze. Serve while still warm.

Note: do not refrigerate if the flan is to be eaten cold.

*Pretty as a picture, this sensational fruit salad
is framed by a light orange sauce.*

Composed fruit salad

Selection of fruit, e.g. strawberries, figs, starfruit
raspberries, kiwi fruit, peaches
Sauce
juice and rind of 2 oranges
3 egg yolks, beaten and strained
dash orange liqueur
caster sugar to taste

Put the orange juice and rind into a saucepan and bring to the boil. Remove from the heat and whisk in the egg yolks until the sauce becomes creamy. Pour into a bowl, then place over a pan of simmering water and continue to whisk until the sauce thickens. Strain the sauce and add the liqueur and sugar to taste. Allow to cool.

Prepare the fruit, slicing the strawberries, starfruit and kiwi and quartering the figs. Arrange the fruit on individual plates and carefully pour the sauce around before serving.

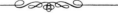

Carrot cake

175ml/6floz corn or sunflower oil
175g/6oz light brown soft sugar
3 eggs
5ml/1 teaspoon vanilla essence
100g/4oz walnuts, chopped
225g/8oz carrots, grated
175g/6oz wholemeal plain flour
5ml/1 teaspoon bicarbonate of soda
5ml/1 teaspoon baking powder
5ml/1 teaspoon cinnamon

Grease and line the bottom of a 20cm/8in deep cake tin. Place the oil, sugar, eggs and vanilla essence in a bowl and beat well. Add the walnuts and carrots, then fold in the dry ingredients.

Turn the mixture into the prepared tin and cook in the oven at 180°C/350°F/gas 4 for 1 hour, or until the cake is risen and firm. Cool on a rack.

Dorset apple cake

175g/6oz sunflower margarine
150g/5oz soft brown muscovado sugar
3 eggs
15ml/1 tablespoon honey
25g/1oz bran
50g/2oz walnuts, chopped
2.5ml/½ teaspoon each of ground cinnamon and cloves
75g/3oz raisins
225g/8oz dessert apples, grated
175g/6oz wholemeal flour
2.5ml/½ teaspoon bicarbonate of soda
7.5ml/1½ teaspoons cream of tartar
Topping
50g/2oz chopped nuts
30ml/2 tablespoons demerara sugar

Beat the margarine and sugar together until soft and creamy. Beat in the eggs, a little at a time, and then add the honey, bran, nuts, spices, raisins and grated apple. Gently fold in the flour, bicarbonate of soda and the cream of tartar.

Pour into a greased and lined 1kg/2lb bread tin and scatter over the topping mixture. Bake in a pre-heated oven at 180°C/350°F/gas 4 for 15 minutes, and then reduce to 170°C/325 °F/gas 3 for a further 1¼ hours.

Serve warm with butter.

*This traditional Sicilian gâteau provides a
special treat that uses ricotta cheese instead of cream.*

136

Sicilian cassata

Cake
4 eggs
225g/8oz light brown soft sugar
225g/8oz sunflower margarine
225g/8oz wholemeal flour
10ml/2 teaspoons baking powder
Filling
750g/1½lb ricotta cheese
175g/6oz caster sugar
75g/3oz plain chocolate, chopped
50g/2oz pistachio nuts, chopped
175g/6oz crystallized fruit
60ml/4 tablespoons orange liqueur

Grease and line with greaseproof paper a 1kg/2lb long loaf tin. Put all the ingredients for the cake into a bowl and beat together for 2 minutes. Turn into the tin and bake at 180°C/350°F/gas 4 for 45 minutes or until risen and golden. Remove from the tin and cool.

Put the cheese and sugar into a bowl and beat together, setting aside one-third in the refrigerator. Stir the chocolate, half the nuts and 100g/4oz of the fruit, chopped, into the remaining mixture. Slice the cake in three horizontally and place the first layer in the loaf tin. Sprinkle with a little of the liqueur. Spread over half of the filling, then repeat the layers finishing with the sponge. Place in the refrigerator for at least 3 hours.

Turn on to a serving plate and spread the reserved cheese over the top and sides. Decorate with the rest of the chopped nuts and the remaining fruit.

Serves 8–10

This dessert is made with wholemeal shortcakes topped with fresh pineapple and low-fat cheese.

Pineapple shortcakes

Biscuits
100g/4oz butter
50g/2oz light brown soft sugar
100g/4oz wholemeal flour
50g/2oz ground rice
Topping
½ small pineapple
175g/6oz fromage frais (low-fat soft cheese)
10ml/2 teaspoons clear honey
few drops of vanilla essence
50g/2oz blanched almonds, chopped and lightly toasted

Cream the butter and sugar together in a bowl. Add the flour and ground rice, and mix until the mixture begins to stick together. Turn out on to a floured surface and knead to make a smooth dough. Roll and cut out large decorative shapes. Place the biscuits on greased baking trays and cook at 180°C/350°F/gas 4 for about 15 minutes until crisp. Allow to cool.

Cut the pineapple into small pieces and arrange them on the shortcakes. Mix together the fromage frais, honey, vanilla essence and half of the nuts. Spoon on to the pineapple, then scatter with the remaining nuts and serve.

A crunchy flapjack case contains cooked apple and dried fruits the colour of autumn to harmonize with the season.

Autumn flan

50g/2oz butter
50g/2oz demerara sugar
45ml/3 tablespoons golden syrup
175g/6oz porridge oats
Filling
225g/8oz cooking apples, peeled, cored and diced
25g/1oz light brown soft sugar
225g/8oz dried fruit salad, soaked overnight
30ml/2 tablespoons marmalade
15ml/1 tablespoon Calvados
25g/1oz blanched almonds, toasted

Heat the butter, demerara sugar and golden syrup gently in a saucepan until the butter has melted. Stir in the oats, then tip into a greased 23cm/9in deep flan tin and spread evenly over the base and sides. Cook at 180°C/350°F/gas 4 for about 30 minutes, or until golden brown. Allow to cool, then remove from the tin.

Put the apple into a pan with 15ml/1 tablespoon water and cook slowly until soft. Remove from the heat, beat in the sugar and allow to cool. Simmer the fruit in its soaking liquid for 10 minutes, then drain and allow to cool.

Spread the cooked apple in the flapjack case and arrange the fruit salad on top. Heat the marmalade and Calvados in a small pan until the marmalade melts, then brush over the fruit. Scatter with blanched almonds.

Note: this is best eaten on the day of making as it will go soggy overnight.

Index

Numerals in *italics* refer to illustrations

Acknowledgements

We would like to thank Sue Jorgensen for taking the
photographs in this book and Lorna Rhodes for
preparing the food for photography.
Our thanks also to the following suppliers
for their kindness in lending items for photography:
Amtico Tiles : laminated tiles
Chinacraft : china and glassware
Croft Bros Ltd : marble
Kilkenny Design : linen, crockery and glassware
Line of Scandinavia : glassware
David Mellor : cutlery, crockery and glassware
Neal Street East : china and fabric
Reject China Shop : china
Wedgwood : china